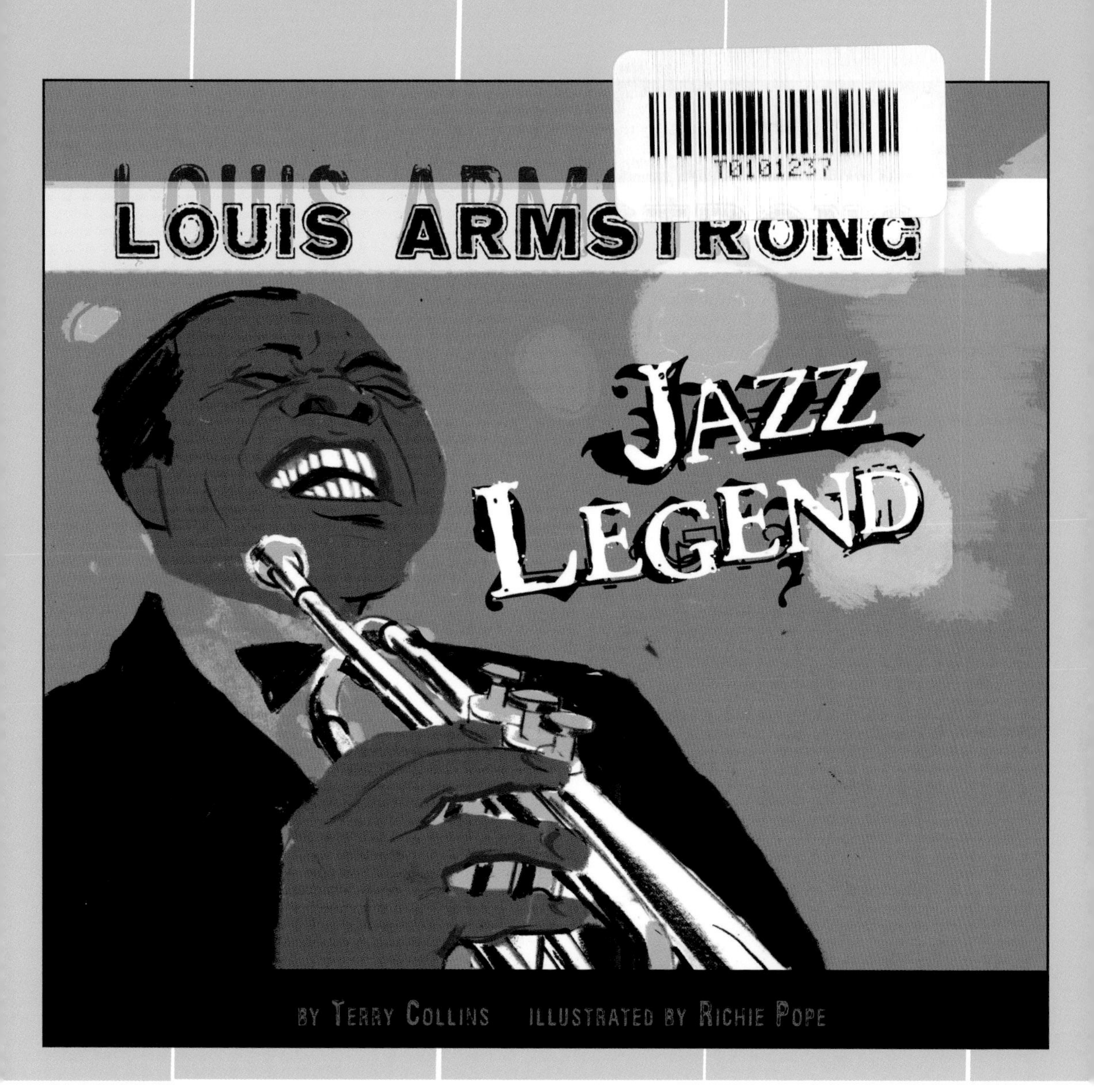

Consultant:
Ricky Riccardi, Archivist
Louis Armstrong House Museum
Queens College, New York

CAPSTONE PRESS
a capstone imprint

Graphic Library is published by Capstone Press,
1710 Roe Crest Drive
North Mankato, Minnesota 56003
www.capstonepub.com

Library of Congress Cataloging-in-Publication Data
Collins, Terry
Louis Armstrong : jazz legend / by Terry Collins.
p. cm. – (Graphic library. American graphic)
Includes bibliographical references and index.
Summary: "Describes the life of Louis Armstrong, focusing on his rise as a pop-culture icon"–Provided by publisher.
ISBN 978-1-4296-8622-8 (library binding)
ISBN 978-1-4296-9336-3 (paperback)
ISBN 978-1-62065-267-1 (ebook PDF)
ISBN 978-1-4765-3068-0 (e-book)
1. Armstrong, Louis, 1901-1971–Juvenile literature. 2. Jazz musicians–United States–Biography–Juvenile literature. I. Title.

ML3930.A75C69 2013
781.65092–dc23 2011049811

Art Director: Nathan Gassman
Editor: Mari Bolte
Production Specialist: Laura Manthe

Direct quotes appear on the following pages in green:
4, 5, 6, 7, 8, 9, 11, 17, from *Satchmo: My Life in New Orleans* by Louis Armstrong (New York: Da Capo Press, Inc., 1986).
10, 12, from *Louis Armstrong: Ambassador Satchmo* by Jean Gay Cornell (Champaign, Ill.: Garrard Publishing Company, 1972).
14, 16, 26, 27, from *Louis Armstrong, In His Own Words* by Louis Armstrong. Edited and With an Introduction by Thomas Brothers (New York: Oxford University Press, 1999).
22, 23, 25, from *Louis Armstrong: An Extravagent Life* by Laurence Bergreen (New York: Broadway Books, 1997).

Photo Credit:
Library of Congress: Prints and Photographs Division, 28

Printed in the United States of America in North Mankato, Minnesota.
082018 000875

TABLE OF CONTENTS

Beth Israel Hospital,
New York City, March 1969
... Louis' condition is serious, Mrs. Armstrong. His heart is weak, and I'm worried about kidney damage.

He's got to start taking better care of himself, Lucille. Louis has to slow down. He isn't a young man anymore.
Now Dr. Zucker, you know how stubborn Louis can be ...

... His whole life and soul centers on singing and blowing that horn.
SCRITCH
SCRITCH
SCRITCH!
Written by Louis Armstrong—ill in his hospital bed.
I was born in New Orleans on a little street called Jane Alley, sometimes called James Alley.

James Alley lies in the very heart of what is called The Battlefield because the toughest characters in town used to live there ...
Ever since I was a small kid, I have always been a great observer.

Of course, on one cold New Year's Eve in 1912, I should have been watching closer.
Please, mister, don't arrest me ... I won't do it no more! Please ... let me go back to Mama.

I was taken to the juvenile court, and then locked up.
CLINK

Louis Armstrong?
Yes, sir.
You're being sent to the Colored Waifs' Home for Boys.

During the New Year's Eve celebration, I had fired my stepfather's pistol over and over into the air.
Making noise for the New Year was an old custom in New Orleans. But not, it seemed, for a 12-year-old colored boy on a public street.
The Waifs' Home was in the country, near a big dairy farm. I, being a city boy, had never seen anything like it.

Captain Jones, who ran things, was a strict man. He drilled us military-style every morning.
SOUND OFF! 1-2!
SOUND OFF! 3-4!

Mr. Alexander taught the boys how to do carpentry, how to garden, and how to build campfires.
Never saw on the line. Cut next to the line to leave material for trimming and finishing.

Mr. Peter Davis taught music.
At first I did not get on very well with Mr. Davis because he did not like the neighborhood I came from.

The little brass band was very good, and Mr. Davis made the boys play a little of every kind of music.
I would sit in a corner and listen, enjoying myself immensely.

Six months passed, and then, one day he asked ...
Louis Armstrong, how would you like to join our brass band?

Mr. Davis started me out on the tambourine ...
... then the bugle ...
... and finally, a few weeks later, the cornet.
I also learned to play the drums.

I got so good at playing the cornet that one day ...
You're going to be the leader of the band, Louis.
The band often got a chance to play at a private picnic or join one of the frequent parades through the streets of New Orleans.

I was fourteen when I was let go from the Home. Part of me didn't want to leave.
I'll never forget what you've done for me, Mr. Davis.
Keep up with your music, son. You've made a fine start.

But I was lucky. I soon found a job working on a coal cart for a Russian-Jewish immigrant family, the Karnofskys.
Stone coal! Nickel a bucket!
On a good day, I'd earn seventy-five cents free and clear. It helped my family pay the bills.

I don't know what would have happened to me without the help of those kind people.
... Ninety-five ... and a nickel makes one dollar.
But Papa Karnofsky, that's too much money.

Use what's left to buy yourself a horn.
How are you going to practice your music if you don't have an instrument?

I wanted to start performing. My friend Buddy Martin said he might have something for me.
My boss is looking for a cornet player. Isn't that what you play?
Yes ... but I don't know if I am good enough to play in a regular band.

Buddy got the gig for me, but now I needed a horn.
Most of the money I earned went to help my folks. Still, with Papa Karnofsky's help, I had scraped together about 10 dollars.
PAWN
SHOP

I looked high and low for a horn, but even the saddest ones were priced too high.

This was my last stop. I had money in my pocket to spend if the price was right.

Maybe, just maybe, my luck would change.
How much is this horn, mister?
Fifteen dollars.
But it's all dented.
Plays just as good with the dents as without.

He was right. The little horn was nothing to look at, but sounded just fine.

Thanks for letting me see it, sir. But I've only got 10 dollars.
Ten bucks, eh?

The pawnshop owner must have seen how much I wanted that horn.

The first night I worked, I made fifteen cents. I spent my nights making music, but I didn't give up my coal wagon job either.
And I was still learning the musician's trade.

When I wasn't playing, I was listening to other musicians.
You sounded great tonight, Joe.
Thanks, kid.
Joe Oliver has always been my inspiration and my idol ... when Joe would get through playing, I'd carry his horn.

Joe gave me cornet lessons.
No, Satchelmouth, try holding your lips like this.

Everyone called me Satchelmouth, which later was shortened to "Satchmo." Some people think they were making fun of me, but I disagree.
My so-called "big mouth" allowed me to play longer and better. It helped with my singing too.

Years passed, and I kept improving. I even became a member of the Tuxedo Brass Band. Everybody wanted to hear me play.
I had many regular gigs, including with orchestras for steamboats on the Mississippi River.

No more hauling coal for nickels. Those days were over.
Joe Oliver had left New Orleans in 1918, and was now up in Chicago doing real swell.

In 1922 he invited me to join his Creole Jazz Band.
I wouldn't have left New Orleans for anyone but "Papa Joe" Oliver.

My opening night at the Lincoln Gardens dance hall was magic. I felt like I was at home.
We cracked down on the first note and that band sounded so good to me ... the first number went down so well we had to take an encore.

After the floor show was over and they went into some dance tunes the crowd yelled:
Let the youngster blow!
I had hit the big time. I was up North with the greats. I was playing with my idol, the King, Joe Oliver.
My boyhood dream had come true at last.

Playing in Chicago was just the beginning. Our band went on tour and I got to see America.
I made some of my first records with Joe Oliver. All of us were thrilled to be recorded at last.
Brunswick
BRUNSWICK
But staying put in someone else's studio meant, I'd never be in control of my music.

In 1924 Joe and I parted as friends. I moved to New York City. I played and recorded with many bands and blues singers.
Still, I missed Chicago. So, I came back, and began recording as the leader of "Louis Armstrong and His Hot Five."

In 1926 we recorded "Heebie Jeebies." I did some scat singing, which proved to be popular.
I got the heebies I got the heebie jeebies And I'm talking about Got the Heebie Jeebie Blues ...

But I wasn't cut out to be a band leader. I wanted to play music, not be the boss.
... and that was Louis Armstrong and his Hot Five with the jazz number, "West End Blues."
I stayed in Chicago and did lots of radio shows.

I even made it to Broadway in an all-black musical review called *Hot Chocolates.*
I ended up recording one of the songs from the show. "Ain't Misbehavin'" by Fats Waller became my best-selling record.
No one to talk with, all by myself, No one to walk with, but I'm happy on the shelf! Ain't misbehavin' ...

I also spent time in California making movies, such as *Pennies From Heaven* with Bing Crosby.
... When the skeleton in the closet started to dance!

In 1948 I appeared on Ed Sullivan's *Talk of the Town* television show for the first time.
Ladies and Gentleman, Mr. Louis Armstrong!

All through the 1930s and 1940s, I watched jazz grow in popularity. People of all kinds were interested in hearing the music.
In 1949 I became the first jazz musician ever to appear on the cover of *Time* magazine.
Old Satchmo on the cover of *Time.* I still can't believe it!

Seems the country was becoming more accepting of who you were.
TIME
TIME
The color of your skin didn't seem as important.

Still, a lot of people felt differently. One night in 1957, I was playing a concert in Knoxville, Tennessee.
The group was wailing on "Back O' Town Blues" when the entire theater shook.
WHA-BOOM!
Some fools from the White Citizens Council tossed a stick of dynamite at the theater.

Guess they didn't like having a black and white audience watching my show together, even if they were segregated. Luckily, no one was hurt.
That's all right, folks, it's just the phone.
HA HA HA HA HA HA
HA HA HA HA HA

I always kept race out of my music. But I believed in the civil rights movement.
chmo' Tells Off Ike,

Later that same year, during the attempt to desegregate in Little Rock, Arkansas, I finally said my piece.
My people ... are not looking for anything. We just want a square shake.
But when I see on television and read about a crowd in Arkansas spitting on a little colored girl, I think I have the right to get sore.

I think President Eisenhower listened.
The president has sent 1,200 National Guardsmen to escort the nine colored students to Central High School here in Little Rock.

In 1960 I toured Africa as part of a four-month trip sponsored by the U.S. State Department.
I was carried into the stadium in the Congo like a visiting king. I even stopped a civil war for a day. Both sides in the Congo Crisis called a temporary truce to hear me perform.

Towards the end of 1963, my manager gave me a song to record from a new Broadway musical.
To be honest, I didn't think much of the tune. I sang it, played a horn solo, and then forgot all about it.
WELL, HELLO, DOLLY! IT'S SO NICE TO HAVE YOU BACK WHERE YOU BELONG ...

On May 9th, 1964, "Hello, Dolly!" went to number one on the charts.
I knocked The Beatles down to number two.

A few years later, and I was singing the song to Miss Barbra Streisand in the movie *Hello, Dolly!*
I was busier than ever, and that was OK with this cat.
People are quick to forget you if you don't keep your name before the public.

Chapter 5 WHAT A WONDERFUL WORLD

As long as you are still doing something interesting and good, you are in business as long as you are breathing.
There's no such thing as on the way out.
I SEE TREES OF GREEN, RED ROSES TOO I SEE THEM BLOOM FOR ME AND YOU AND I THINK TO MYSELF ... WHAT A WONDERFUL WORLD.
Louis Armstrong continued to give performances around the world. In March 1971, he played a final two week series of shows at the Waldorf-Astoria in New York City. On July 6, 1971, the great Satchmo died peacefully in his sleep.

Satchmo's Legacy

LOUIS ARMSTRONG was born in New Orleans, Louisiana, on August 4, 1901. He was the only son of Willie and Mary Ann Armstrong. His father abandoned the family soon after Louis was born. Louis' early life was one of extreme poverty. His family lived in the worst part of New Orleans, in a neighborhood called The Battlefield.

Louis was forced to grow up quickly. He quit school in the third grade. He took any and all odd jobs to help support his family. An energetic boy with a wide smile, Louis later recalled enjoying his childhood despite the circumstances. He also remembered hearing jazz music playing from nearby clubs and dance halls.

As time passed, he formed a quartet that sang on corners for pennies. Louis knew that one day he would make a living from music. However, his first real training came in 1913, when he was sent to the Waifs' Home.

After his release from the home, Louis began his professional music career. His trademark gravelly voice and playful delivery was as unmistakable as his trumpet playing. By using his quick sense of humor and boyish smile, Louis grew in popularity with audiences both black and white.

He made film, radio, and TV appearances on a regular basis. He began touring the world, often serving as an unofficial "good will ambassador" for the United States. In the decades to come, he would be known to a younger generation more for his singing abilities than as an instrumentalist.

With this later success in life came increasing hospital stays and ailing periods of recovery at home. Despite health setbacks, Louis continued to tour and perform up until his death on July 6, 1971.

GLOSSARY

blues (BLOOZ)—a style of slow, sad music created by African-Americans

civil rights (SI-vil RYTS)—the rights that all people have to freedom and equal treatment under the law

encore (AHN-kor)—a song played after a band ends the main part of a concert

gig (GIG)—a live performance in front of an audience

jazz (JAZ)—a lively, rhythmical type of music in which players often make up their own tunes and add new notes in unexpected places

orchestra (OR-kuh-struh)—a large group of musicians who play their instruments together

pawnshop (PAWN-shop)—a shop where people can leave a valuable item in return for a loan; the item is returned if the loan is paid back, otherwise items are sold to other customers

scat (SKAT)—a type of singing in which the singer imitates a jazz instrument vocally without words

segregate (SEG-ruh-gate)—to keep people of different races apart in schools and other public places

READ MORE

Fahlenkamp-Merrell, Kindle. *Louis Armstrong.* Journey to Freedom. Mankato, Minn.: Child's World, 2010.

Tougas, Shelley. *Little Rock Girl 1957: How a Photograph Changed the Fight for Integration.* Captured History. Mankato, Minn.: Compass Point Books, 2012.

INTERNET SITES

FactHound offers a safe, fun way to find Internet sites related to this book. All of the sites on FactHound have been researched by our staff.

Here's all you do:

Visit www.facthound.com

Type in this code: 9781429686228

Check out projects, games and lots more at **www.capstonekids.com**